Traffic Sheds, Rural Highway Capacity, and Growth Management

Lane Kendig
with
Stephen Tocknell, AICP

The Traffic Shed Concept 1

Shortcomings in Growth Management Strategies for Rural Areas 3

Using Traffic Sheds as an Alternative Growth Management Strategy
   in Rural Areas 5

Traffic Shed Regulation 7

Seven Development Options under Traffic Shed Regulation 9

A Case Study: Williamson County, Tennessee 17

Other Communities Using Traffic Sheds 21

Summary 23

Traffic Sheds, Rural Highway Capacity, and Growth Management

Contrary to conventional wisdom, many rural communities located on the fringes of metropolitan areas share a thorny traffic problem with their urban counterparts: the road network simply cannot support additional development. Rural roads may be narrow, winding, or unpaved, sometimes featuring one-lane bridges or even fords—all characteristics that merit a substandard rating. The problem is not limited to areas where the network has an irregular configuration; it also occurs where the road pattern is a grid or partial grid configuration. The characteristics of the individual road and network pattern result in some rural communities having road networks that are simply inadequate.

While planners may expect road network failure in rural counties that pay scant attention to planning or zoning matters, a regulatory system does not guarantee immunity from the problem. Many zoned communities with such problems share a common large-lot zoning pattern that allows residential development across large areas of the community. The lot-size minimums range from one to five acres. Neither zoning nor subdivision controls can protect a community from network failure if such large lots result in densities that do not relate to network capacity. Exemptions to subdivision controls that promote strip development and a lack of curb-cut restrictions are other examples of unintended regulatory consequences that can lead to growth beyond the rural road network's capacity.

While many rural communities use large-lot zoning to promote farmland preservation, in reality it often results in low-density residential development. Where low-density residential zoning exists at the outer edges of a metropolitan area, the first stages of development are single lots carved off road frontages or development of small, 3- to 10-lot subdivisions. The result: a pattern of scattered development throughout the area, necessitating widespread public improvements.

The cost of improving a large percentage of these rural roads, however, exceeds the fiscal resources of most rural counties. In some cases, fiscal conservatism is to blame for failing to make needed upgrades to roads. In other cases, however, the roads have not been upgraded because they were perfectly adequate for the rural farm community. In yet other cases, scenic or historic concerns mandate that the road pattern be maintained in the face of encroaching development.

THE TRAFFIC SHED CONCEPT

Using the concept of a traffic shed to do transportation network analysis may provide an answer to these problems. This concept will be new to most planners, although it is being used as a regulatory tool in Williamson

1

County, Tennessee. The traffic shed has been used in planning in Loudoun County, Virginia; Nantucket, Massachusetts; Fayette County, Kentucky; Woodford County, Kentucky; and Miami County, Kansas. Blue Grass Tomorrow, a nonprofit planning organization based in Lexington, Kentucky is recommending traffic sheds in their seven-county plan.

Somewhat analogous to the familiar concept of a watershed, the traffic shed concept stems from the premise that rural residents use the township or county roadways to get to major arterials (typically state or federal highways) upon which they commute to their jobs. It is essential to the traffic shed concept that the commutation pattern on the arterials be largely unidirectional. Thus, the flow of traffic down the rural road to a major arterial is similar to the flow of water downstream from a creek to a river—hence, the term "traffic shed." These major roads may be as much as 10 miles apart, requiring travelers to drive up to five miles on a rural road to reach the arterial. The traffic shed concept can be applied as both an analytical system and a regulatory approach. Implementing the system requires only that planners calculate road capacity using standard transportation methodology.

If traffic flows in various directions (into the central city and circumferentially), as it does in many suburban communities, a trip distribution program and transportation model, rather than the traffic shed model, are needed.

As shown in Figure 1, the rural road network has two components: rural highways functioning as major arterials and rural farm-to-market roads connecting to the main roads. Nearly all rush-hour trips entail commuters using a rural road to access the nearest arterial that leads to their jobs in the nearby city. Thus, the rural roads can be treated like a first-order stream draining to the larger stream. Like a watershed, the traffic shed is the land area that generates the traffic that flows to the road. If there are no physical constraints, traffic shed boundaries would be halfway between two roads. Railroads, streams, and ridge lines are physical features that can warp the boundary between two traffic sheds. As is formulated in the latest edition of the Transportation Research Board (TRB) *Highway Capacity Manual*, road capacity is based on width and number of lanes, percent of road where there is no passing, directionality of travel, and proximity of obstructions to the pavement. Two other factors that may need to be factored into the manual's methodology when considering rural road networks are one-lane roads and differentiations based on type of paving. Substandard widths and problems with the vertical and horizontal alignment of the roads, whether paved or unpaved, can limit the ability to pass slow-moving vehicles (particularly large farm vehicles) and decrease capacity, and must also be considered.

Determining road capacity is the first critical element of conducting a traffic shed analysis. The second critical element is determining the traffic shed area for each rural road. Knowing the area of the traffic shed and the capacity of the receiving rural road makes it possible to determine the amount of

The traffic shed concept can be applied as both an analytical system and a regulatory approach. Implementing the system requires only that planners calculate road capacity using standard transportation methodology.

Figure 1. The Rural Road Network

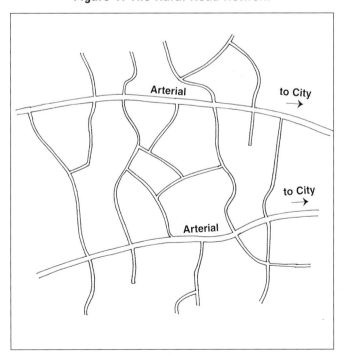

development that can be supported overall. The amount of supportable development is expressed in term of traditional density measures (i.e., dwelling units per acre). Readily available, per-unit, peak-hour trip generation factors from the Institute of Transportation Engineer's *Trip Generation* manual can be used to convert trips on a one-trip-per-one-dwelling-unit basis. (Note: Nearly all development within the traffic shed will be residential.) Thus, dividing the traffic shed area by the number of dwelling units yields the number of acres required per dwelling unit. Inverting this ratio (i.e., dividing the number of dwelling units by the traffic shed area) yields dwelling units per acre.

As noted above, the critical elements affecting the results of the analysis are road capacity and traffic shed area. Inadequate roads minimize capacity, while improvements increase capacity. For any road, a large traffic shed will result in lower densities than will a smaller traffic shed. Because of this fact, a viable strategy for large landowners with arterial frontage is to build a new road, thus shrinking the size of the applicable traffic shed. (See Figure 2.) A new traffic shed must be mapped, its area deducted from the parent traffic shed, and both sheds' capacities recalculated accordingly. Note that this approach increases the capacity for the developer and the landowners in the rest of the traffic shed.

The traffic shed analysis is also a planning tool that can educate officials about the relationship between planning, zoning, and road capacity. Where road capacity is limited, the two major options for avoiding congestion or dangerous conditions are to build new infrastructure or to limit density. This information can inform capital improvement or planning debates as to the nature of the problem and possible solutions. If nothing else, the traffic shed is a useful analytic tool that can be applied to growth management issues where transportation is a critical element.

SHORTCOMINGS IN GROWTH MANAGEMENT STRATEGIES FOR RURAL AREAS

What can be done to get control of situations in which growth is stressing the road system and the community is falling behind in providing new or improved roads? While some very obvious solutions to the problem of inadequate infrastructure and growth exist, they are often difficult to implement. A rural county planner's logical approach is to recommend a growth management plan that contains development within an urban growth area. Concentrating growth in a small fraction of the rural area greatly reduces the miles of needed road improvements and, thus, the public cost of development. Even though the growth in rural counties may appear immense when expressed in terms of percentage increase over time, in absolute terms, the total amount of rural development is probably modest enough to fit in a fairly compact area. Under typical growth management plans, the remainder of the county not designated for infrastructure improvements and future growth is zoned for agriculture or low-density residential (e.g., one unit per 30 to 40 acres). In this scenario, the road network's capacity to accommodate growth can be sustained in part because little or no residential development actually occurs at such low densities.

The urban growth boundary concept is so simple, obvious, and rational that it should be a standard tool used by rural fringe counties everywhere. Reality shows us that strong growth management systems are the excep-

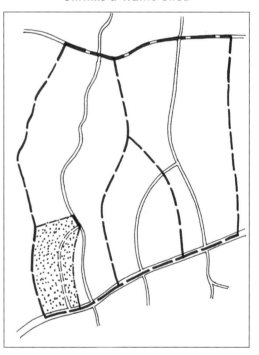

Figure 2. Road Construction Shrinks a Traffic Shed

The urban growth boundary concept is so simple, obvious, and rational that it should be a standard tool used by rural fringe counties everywhere. Reality shows us that strong growth management systems are the exception rather than the rule.

tion rather than the rule. In fact, most rural counties with zoning have a rural district that permits residential uses on one- to five-acre lots. This density is spread liberally throughout the county and becomes the default plan. Even counties with plans touting their strong growth management orientation often have zoning that permits one-half-acre to five-acre lots outside the urban areas. For example, one county with such a plan not only permits one- to three-acre lots everywhere, but also exempts lots with three or more acres from subdivision if the lot frontage is greater than 150 feet. The result is that most development is stripped off on three-acre lots to avoid subdivision review. The idea of downzoning much of a county to steer development into an urban growth boundary has not fared well, except where this type of planning is mandated. Faced with difficulty implementing urban growth limits and land-use solutions, planners throughout the country have tested other strategies.

Most suburban planners have turned to impact fee systems. Impact fees work best in cities or high- growth or heavily populated counties. These communities experience enough growth that the revenues generated from impact fees actually pay for major transportation improvements. Heavily developed suburban counties (i.e., counties that are more than half built out) may also find that impact fees meet objectives. Road impact fees are least likely to fulfill expectations in suburban and exurban counties with substantial remaining development potential. In the absence of urban growth boundary controls, sprawl results in the need for more improved lane miles than the impact fee system revenue stream can finance.

A quick reality check confirms the futility of relying on impact fees in a growing rural county. First, calculate how many miles of road might be improved over a 20-year period and then allocate the cost to the projected residential growth. The resulting road impact fees will be so high that they will have a severe impact on landowners and the market.

A quick reality check confirms the futility of relying on impact fees in a growing rural county. First, calculate how many miles of road might be improved over a 20-year period and then allocate the cost to the projected residential growth. The resulting road impact fees will be so high that they will have a severe impact on landowners and the market. In Miami County, Kansas, where 80 percent of the roads were gravel, the road impact fee required to make needed improvements over 20 years equaled about $30,000 per lot. This figure, while defensible in terms of planners' abilities to document the costs beyond a reasonable doubt, is so high that it stretches credibility and becomes legally suspect. Experience indicates that, for road impact fees to succeed in rural counties, they must be used in concert with an urban growth boundary. Impact fees alone are inadequate to address rural road problems.

Adequate facilities ordinances, another growth management tool, are intended to maintain development at a level consistent with an area's infrastructure. In this system, development stops when the capacity of the road is exceeded. Adequate facilities ordinances are based on a first-come, first-served philosophy. As long as capacity remains, the landowner can obtain permits as allowed under current zoning. Once capacity is reached, no more permits are issued. Since the possibility of being refused permission to build strikes many landowners as draconian, adequate facilities ordinances are rare. Moreover, as the developers exhaust available capacity, the adequate facilities approach forces them to search for land in the urban fringe where capacity remains. In Florida, the concurrency management system resulted in development of more remote areas, forcing premature sprawl. This was contrary to public policy goals and actually worked against compact development and infill in urban areas.

To develop alternative approaches to the growth management techniques described above, the factors impelling rural areas to resist such techniques must be understood. First, residents and local elected officials in rural counties are often very leery of zoning—even if it permits large-lot development. When zoning for agricultural use or growth management is proposed, the resistance to zoning increases. Agricultural zoning that limits density to, for example, one house per 30 to 50 acres portends significantly lower land values than anticipated under a one- to five-acre lot, low-density, residential zone. Altering property values provokes a very strong emotional response from property owners. County commissioners are often very reluctant to impose severe restrictions on fellow farmers and landowners they have known all their lives. Second, land-use control solutions tread on the belief widely cherished by landowners and property rights activists that the market will solve the problem. But the market solution to solving a road capacity shortage is to develop land in outlying areas where capacity remains. And because new development begets even more development, eventually capacity shortages arise in outlying areas, and the cycle continues. So, from a planning standpoint, there is not an acceptable, cost-efficient market solution to solving the problem of inadequate road capacity.

USING TRAFFIC SHEDS AS AN ALTERNATIVE GROWTH MANAGEMENT STRATEGY IN RURAL AREAS

Traffic shed analysis is worthy of consideration in counties where standard growth management techniques have been met with resistance and where congestion problems are starting to emerge. The traffic shed concept is, first, a means of analysis. If the analysis tells the planner that traffic on existing roads is nearing or has exceeded available capacity, then measures to minimize or redirect development may be considered. The results of the analysis are useful in persuading local officials about the need to address growth issues.

Unlike urban growth boundaries, the traffic shed does not require that the land be downzoned. The local zoning, however poorly it addresses the growth management issue, can be left in place. Instead, traffic sheds work as a performance standard overlay on the zoning classification, just as soils may limit the ability to maintain density where septic tanks are used.

Consider a traffic shed of 920 vacant acres. A capacity analysis of the road network, based on the principles in the *Highway Capacity Manual*, determines that, if the desired LOS (level of service) is B, the road in the traffic shed can support 419 trips. Figure 3A illustrates the calculation. The conditions of the road indicated are:

• percent of road where no passing is allowed: 20 percent;

• lane width: 10 feet;

• obstructions: within two feet of the pavement; and

• the road is paved.

The example assumes a partially developed traffic shed with 38 trips so that the remaining capacity is 381 trips. The directional split was indicated at 60/40 with 2 percent truck traffic. If this 920-acre traffic shed is zoned for one-acre lots with a density of 0.78 dwelling units per acre, the capacity would be 717 dwelling units. (The density of 0.78, assumes full one-acre lots with 150 feet of frontage, a 66-foot right-of-way, detention or open space consuming 5 percent of the site, and an average inefficiency of 5 percent. Inefficiency occurs on cul-de-sac and corner lots that are typically

Using traffic sheds as opposed to urban growth boundary or adequate public facilities provisions allows each landowner to receive a fair share of the traffic shed's capacity.

larger than the minimum. There may also be other factors leading to inefficiency in the developer's ability to get lots that are exactly 43,560 square feet in area.)

Given these numbers, the traffic shed would support about 717 dwelling units (920 acres x .78 dwelling units). As already noted, the roads have a capacity for only 381 remaining trips in their current state, or approximately 0.41 dwelling units per acre. Unless or until the roads are improved, the overlay reduces the density from .78 dwelling units per acre to .415 dwelling units per acre, a reduction of 52 percent. Figure 3B contains a second run of the traffic shed model which indicates that, if the developer widened the road to provide a lane width of 12 feet, the remaining capacity would be increased to 462 vehicles per hour, and a density of .502 dwelling units per acre.

Figure 3A. Traffic Shed Highway Capacity Analysis, 920 Acres, 10-foot Roadway

Enter Highway Service and Alignment Data

Level of Service	2	Enter: 1=A; 2=B; 3=C; 4=D; 5=E;
Percent No Passing	2	Enter: 1=0%; 2=20%; 3=40%; 4=60%; 5=80%; 6=100%
Lane Width	3	Enter: 1=12ft; 2=11ft; 3=10ft; 4=9ft; 5=8ft; 6=7ft; 7=1 lane
Obstructions	3	Enter: 1=6ft; 2=4ft; 3=2ft; 4=0ft
paved?	1	1=Yes; 2=No

Enter

Existing Volume	38	Enter No. vehicles per hour
Directional Split	2	Enter: 1=50/50; 2=60/40; 3=70/30; 4=80/20
Percent Trucks	0.02	Enter % as decimal
Percent RV's	0.00	Enter % as decimal
Percent Buses	0.00	Enter % as decimal

Traffic Shed Area	920	Enter in Acres
Select Land Use	1	Enter Land Use Number

Residential 1=SF; 2=Town/Condo; 3=Apts; 4=Apts 4st+
Commercial 5=Retail; 6=Foodstore; 7=Restuarant
Shopping Center 8=neighborhood; 9=community; 10=Regional
Service 11=Office; 12=Medical; 13=Bank
Employment 14=Industry; 15=office/industry; 16=Warehouse
Highway 17=Fat Food; 18=Vehicle Sales; 19=Convenience Mart

Road Capacity	419 vehicles per hour
Remaining Capacity	381 vehicles per hour
Selected Use:	single family
Maximum Intensity:	0.415 DU's/acre
	2.411691 acres per unit

Figure 3B. Traffic Shed Highway Capacity Analysis, 920 Acres, 12-foot Roadway

Enter Highway Service and Alignment Data

Level of Service	2	Enter: 1=A; 2=B; 3=C; 4=D; 5=E;
Percent No Passing	2	Enter: 1=0%; 2=20%; 3=40%; 4=60%; 5=80%; 6=100%
Lane Width	1	Enter: 1=12ft; 2=11ft; 3=10ft; 4=9ft; 5=8ft; 6=7ft; 7=1 lane
Obstructions	3	Enter: 1=6ft; 2=4ft; 3=2ft; 4=0ft
paved?	1	1=Yes; 2=No

Enter

Existing Volume	38	Enter No. vehicles per hour
Directional Split	2	Enter: 1=50/50; 2=60/40; 3=70/30; 4=80/20
Percent Trucks	0.02	Enter % as decimal
Percent RV's	0.00	Enter % as decimal
Percent Buses	0.00	Enter % as decimal

Traffic Shed Area	920	Enter in Acres
Select Land Use	1	Enter Land Use Number

Residential 1=SF; 2=Town/Condo; 3=Apts; 4=Apts 4st+
Commercial 5=Retail; 6=Foodstore; 7=Restuarant
Shopping Center 8=neighborhood; 9=community; 10=Regional
Service 11=Office; 12=Medical; 13=Bank
Employment 14=Industry; 15=office/industry; 16=Warehouse
Highway 17=Fat Food; 18=Vehicle Sales; 19=Convenience Mart

Road Capacity	500 vehicles per hour
Remaining Capacity	462 vehicles per hour
Selected Use:	single family
Maximum Intensity:	0.502 DU's/acre
	1.992771 acres per unit

Using traffic sheds as opposed to urban growth boundary or adequate public facilities provisions allows each landowner to receive a fair share of the traffic shed's capacity. Capacity is allocated on a pro rata basis, so that the owner of 2 percent of the land (i.e., 18 acres) receives 2 percent of the shed capacity. The owner of 24 percent receives 24 percent of the capacity. Every landowner is treated equally. None is prohibited from developing, and no property is downzoned in comparison to other sites.

The performance basis of the traffic shed is also designed to provide additional options to the landowner. In areas governed by an urban growth boundary, some land would be zoned for one-acre lots, while other areas might be downzoned to 30-acre lots to match the carrying capacity of the road network and to meet other objectives. With adequate public facil-

Every landowner is treated equally. None is prohibited from developing, and no property is downzoned in comparison to other sites.

ities provisions, the first developers who could secure allocated capacity would get to build while others would be prohibited until the road system was improved and could support more trips. In either of these scenarios, which allocate allowable development on a first-come, first-served basis, 42 percent of the landowners would see their development opportunities limited in some manner.

TRAFFIC SHED REGULATION

Presenting the traffic shed approach to planning commissioners and elected officials in rural areas is made easier through the use of comparisons. Many understand and are comfortable with other resource and capacity-based regulations (e.g., soil-based regulations prohibiting building permit issuance or subdivision approval when a landowner cannot get an approved septic system). Similarly, farmers and rural landowners understand capacity-based pricing systems. Farmers buy land based on its crop production potential and regularly pay less for land with lower productivity. The traffic shed analysis provides an accurate measure of the capacity of the road network within a traffic shed. Thus, these comparisons are useful for elected officials who want to solve the problem but fear adopting restrictive zoning regulations.

The traffic shed approach also derives appeal from its congruity with the market's invisible hand. Property rights activists and landowners often praise the free market system as a means of achieving society's desired goals. A regulatory system that is based on market forces is more difficult to assail than a typical command-and-control system. While the traffic shed approach uses an analysis that may result in limited capacity for future development, it has advantages over impact fees and adequate facilities ordinances. For example, the traffic shed and the implementing regulations never have to say No to a developer. The traffic shed approach is based on small-area capacity restrictions, so not all areas are equally restricted. Furthermore, impact fees, which can be exorbitant in a sparsely developed area, need not be considered. In the traffic shed approach, landowners and developers are simply forced to incorporate into their economic decision making the adequacy and costs of the road serving the property.

Market systems are very good at promoting informed economic decisions. Nearly everybody understands the concept of getting more for less. Rational people attempt to get more for their scarce resources and avoid paying more for less. Taxpayers are no exception. They are motivated to prevent government from squandering scarce public resources. There is one major problem with the market as it applies to assigning value to land: it fails to account for the costs associated with numerous planning problems, such as inadequate roads. For the market to work from the standpoint of public service provision, it must be able to incorporate into the price the value of the public infrastructure and the costs of expanding it. While the real estate market attributes value to proximity to major roads and destinations, the cost of improving roads is a governmental market decision. To use the analogy we have employed throughout this argument, when government stringently enforces septic tank rules for lots with unsuitable soils, the real estate market prices the land accordingly. Moreover, the knowledgeable buyer will not purchase land that cannot get development approval. Because rural officials are comfortable with this notion, it is not difficult to get them to understand that, if land was accessible only by crossing a ford, there should also be development limits.

The traffic shed approach also derives appeal from its congruity with the market's invisible hand. Property rights activists and landowners often praise the free market system as a means of achieving society's desired goals. A regulatory system that is based on market forces is more difficult to assail than a typical command-and-control system.

There is one major problem with the market as it applies to assigning value to land: it fails to account for the costs associated with numerous planning problems, such as inadequate roads. For the market to work from the standpoint of public service provision, it must be able to incorporate into the price the value of the public infrastructure and the costs of expanding it.

In a free market, a landowner and a developer enter into a willing buyer/seller relationship, and land is sold at a price both consider fair given expectations about profit potential associated with the development opportunity. The developer's sale of the finished unit to a home buyer is similarly dictated by price and value considerations for the home and lot. None of the parties in either sale usually consider the lack of adequate roads. Developers who can buy cheap, rural land lacking good roads can often make more money than their counterparts who purchase land in a more valuable area where services are adequate. In other words, conventional zoning may, in fact, encourage the market forces that result in the building of houses in inadequately served locations. Home buyers, enchanted with the rural location and seduced by evidence that they are getting a much bigger home and lot than they could get for the same price in a suburban development with adequate roads, will often look past the issue of adequate roads. Too often, these buyers do not think of the disadvantages associated with the inadequate road, let alone demand an appropriate discount that would compensate for the shortcomings of the infrastructure and, therefore, reduce the profits associated with exurban residential development. Once they move in, these home buyers identify themselves as voters and taxpayers rather than as housing consumers. Thus, instead of pursuing the developer or the farmer from whom they purchased, they turn to the county commissioners and demand adequate roads. If the real estate market fails to consider a factor such as inadequate roads, no price is attached and market forces cannot solve the problem.

The solution lies in using the zoning system to ensure that the real estate market accounts for roads. Since the traffic shed system apportions the road capacity equally to all landowners in a traffic shed and the road capacity itself is determined using standard, defensible methodologies, the system imposes a development constraint derived in a rational and scientific manner that is expressed in a manner the real estate market is equipped to incorporate into price: allowable density.

In a traffic shed system, the basic zoning standards (e.g., lot size) are not changed. Instead, the zoning ordinance is modified to include a performance overlay that indicates the amount of development permitted given the roadway carrying capacity of each traffic shed. The overlay requires that the results of the traffic shed analysis modify the density. The traffic shed analysis is generally conducted on a communitywide basis at the time of zoning ordinance adoption; landowners need not complete their own analyses. The community should periodically update the traffic shed data as new traffic counts become available or as road improvements boost capacity, leading to an increase in the permitted density. If the county improves a road, the landowners reap the benefit; however, the community as a whole also benefits because the system induces development within the improved traffic shed where the county believes it can best accommodate growth.

Another advantage of the traffic shed is that it permits the landowner or developer to consider a wide range of alternatives. A landowner or developer can price improvements and determine if the investment in new facilities will pay for themselves in terms of a more profitable development. If the road investment can be economically justified, it behooves the developer to make the improvement to gain additional capacity and density. Moreover, other landowners in the improved traffic shed are compensated for the impacts of the project; they, too, will reap additional capacity and

Another advantage of the traffic shed is that it permits the landowner or developer to consider a wide range of alternatives. A landowner or developer can price improvements and determine if the investment in new facilities will pay for themselves in terms of a more profitable development. If the road investment can be economically justified, it behooves the developer to make the improvement to gain additional capacity and density.

density. On the other hand, if the economics are unworkable, the landowner and developer must rethink the deal. Thus, the traffic shed makes roads part of the real estate market equation, facilitating a decision on whether to build in a given location. That decision will not be too different from a similar determination imposed by planners in defining an urban growth boundary plan.

SEVEN DEVELOPMENT OPTIONS UNDER TRAFFIC SHED REGULATION

How does the traffic shed work? First, equality is essential; the landowners must receive their fair share of the available capacity. If, for example, the road will support 300 additional peak-hour trips, then the traffic shed will permit construction of 300 additional homes, assuming one trip per household during peak travel times. The capacity and area of the traffic shed determine the permitted density. In a traffic shed containing 600 acres, the density is one house per two acres or 0.5 dwelling units per acre (300 trips divided by 600 acres = .5 dwelling units per acre). In a much larger traffic shed with 6,000 acres, the density is 0.05 dwelling units per acre (300 trips divided by 6,000 acres = .05 dwelling units per acre). In a Kansas community where this analysis was applied in the development of a comprehensive plan, the traffic sheds served by mostly unpaved section line roads had densities ranging from one home per six acres to one home per 160 acres. Faced with such inadequate roads, communities typically install a floor so that density does not fall below a certain level. Usually an agricultural zoning density of one home per 20 to 40 acres is appropriate. Williamson County, Tennessee, used a five-acre lot as the threshold density.

The analysis applied to each traffic shed (or the minimum density floor) represents a performance overlay. The market element is achieved by the traffic shed capacity calculation and the development options given the landowner. If all the system did was limit development to a lower density, it would be difficult to distinguish it from zoning techniques used to implement an urban growth limit. However, the traffic shed provides a range of options for the landowner and market to evaluate.

1. *Make road improvements.* If a landowner improves the rural road by widening it, the capacity of the road increases. As a result of the enhanced capacity, the total number of dwelling units permitted in the traffic shed will grow. Whether the cost of the improvement will be paid back by the sale of more homes is determined via a conventional market analysis. The developer, banker, or landowner can each weigh the value of increasing density against the cost of the road improvement. The result of the market analysis will reflect comparative sales potential, just as it would with a government-imposed downzoning in an urban growth boundary. A developer with land located far from an improved road would have very large capital costs and would not get a loan (Figure 4, SiteA). The landowner with property nearly contiguous to an arterial could afford to improve the road, and thus gain increased density (Figure 4, Site B). Similarly, the developer who must provide a bridge to increase capacity will have to overcome a much higher cost than would apply to a parcel without this constraint.

Figure 4.

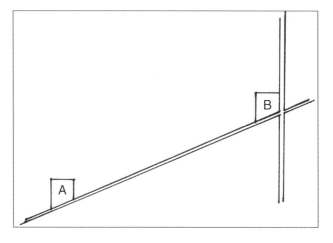

2. *Build out at overlay density.* If the owner wants to develop, but road improvement costs cannot be justified by the return on sales, the landowner can build out at the overlay density. Under this option, the landowner uses the entire site for development. For example, with underlying five-acre zoning with a traffic shed density of one house per 20 acres, the developer would market five 20-acre lots (Figure 5A), instead of the 20 five-acre lots permitted by the underlying zoning (Figure 5B). The landowner and developer reach the market decision that this is a viable economic transaction agreeing to a price that both can accept. In this option, they forgo any future development potential and accept the limited overlay density.

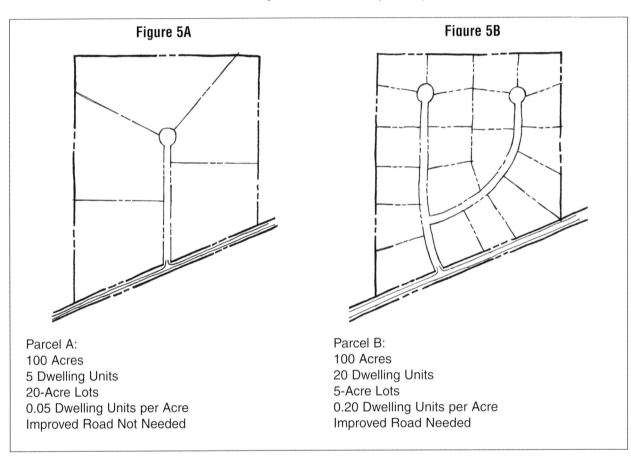

Figure 5A

Figure 5B

Parcel A:
100 Acres
5 Dwelling Units
20-Acre Lots
0.05 Dwelling Units per Acre
Improved Road Not Needed

Parcel B:
100 Acres
20 Dwelling Units
5-Acre Lots
0.20 Dwelling Units per Acre
Improved Road Needed

3. *Use the overlay density and reserve for future development.* This option is similar to Option 2, except that, in selecting a development pattern, land is reserved for future development. The developer builds as allowed under the base zoning district but limits the project to the density allowed under the overlay district. For example, with underlying five-acre zoning with a traffic shed density of one house per 20 acres, the developer would build five of the 20 lots the underlying zoning would permit (Figure 6A), reserving the remainder of the site for future development should the capacity of the traffic shed be increased (Figure 6B). The advantage of this option is that the developer/landowner gets initial short-term profits from the sale. The initial development gives the developer money to pay off acquisition costs. The developer also has the option to use this money to fund improvements to allow further development of the traffic shed. Or she or he can wait for the

county to improve the roads. This option also allows for cluster development or other site planning techniques that include open space preservation. The developer is engaging in initial development to pay for long-term speculation. Clearly, this strategy works best if the initial development provides the needed funds to make the improvement, or when government improvement is likely.

4. *No sale.* The developer always has the option of not buying the land. Landowners do not have to sell. The market analysis that includes the cost of road improvements cuts down on speculative rural develop-

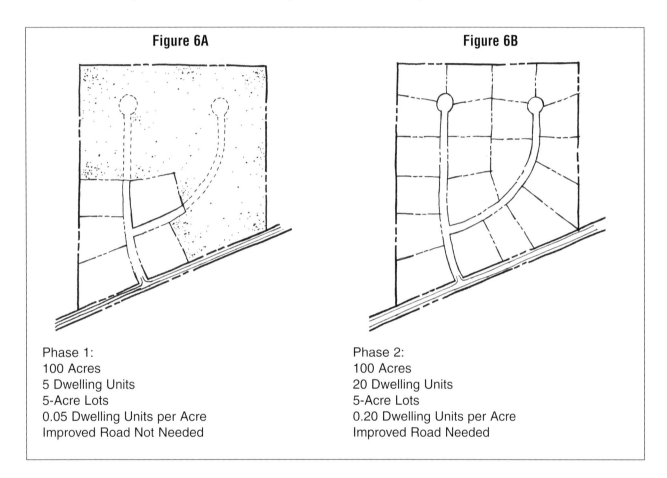

Figure 6A

Phase 1:
100 Acres
5 Dwelling Units
5-Acre Lots
0.05 Dwelling Units per Acre
Improved Road Not Needed

Figure 6B

Phase 2:
100 Acres
20 Dwelling Units
5-Acre Lots
0.20 Dwelling Units per Acre
Improved Road Needed

ment. In normal large-lot zoning, there is a big financial reward for some developer/speculator who buys cheaper rural land and leaves the road or infrastructure improvements to the county. Under the traffic shed, this form of speculation is no longer available. Where the cost of improvements is far more than the savings in land acquisition, the developer will be unwilling to buy. This outcome resembles what happens when a landowner asks too much for a piece of land—it goes unsold.

5. *Adjust the deal.* Another option entails bargaining. If the developer cannot afford to buy and make a profit, the developer may decide to offer a much lower price for all the land or seek to buy only a portion of the land. The landowner can accept the revised price (Options 2 or 3), or the landowner can reject the offer (Option 4). (See Figure 7.) This illus-

trates the workings of a market to adjust for the impact of road improvement costs.

6. *Choice in development patterns.* The first five options all work without any change to the underlying zoning of one- to five-acre conventional, single-family lots and a generally conventional pattern of develop-

Figure 7

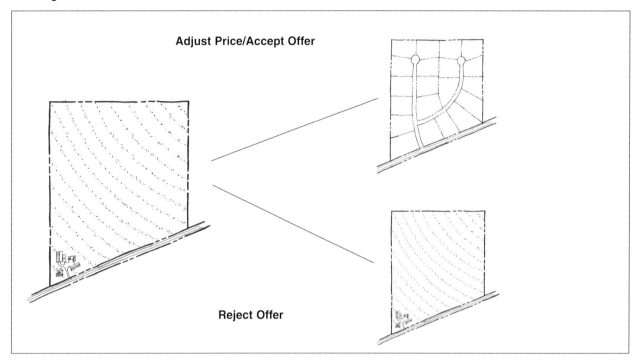

Adjust Price/Accept Offer

Reject Offer

ment. The traffic shed is recommended for use with performance zoning in which the landowner would have several permitted development patterns—conventional single-family, cluster single-family, or planned (a cluster pattern permitting all types of dwelling units). Options 2 and 3 can be enhanced by selecting one of the several forms of clustering. Very low-density clusters with high open-space ratios offer a great advantage in that they can permit farming of the remaining acreage. Cluster development is more profitable for the landowner, because the farm use remains after the development potential is used. If the traffic shed calculation would permit only one house per 20 acres, clustering houses on one-acre lots would preserve between 90 and 95 percent of a site for agricultural use, and three-acre lots would preserve between 80 and 85 percent of the site. (Figures 8A, B, and C.) This scenario results in higher total value of the property because the landowner receives the development value in cash and continues to receive the income from the farm operation. If the landowner does the development and cuts out the developer, the profits from this option are increased.

The developer may also achieve an advantage from using the cluster options. People who move to rural areas are essentially "borrowing" views of nearby farmland. The rural life style is attractive, but typically impermanent—as the adjoining field is subdivided and road frontage stripped off, the rural character is lost. Clustering permits the developer to market the site as having the desired rural character. In some cases, this will enhance the value of the lots, and this means higher returns under any restricted option.

Because of the benefits clustering provides, it is recommended that a small density bonus (perhaps 10 to 40 percent) be given to such devel-

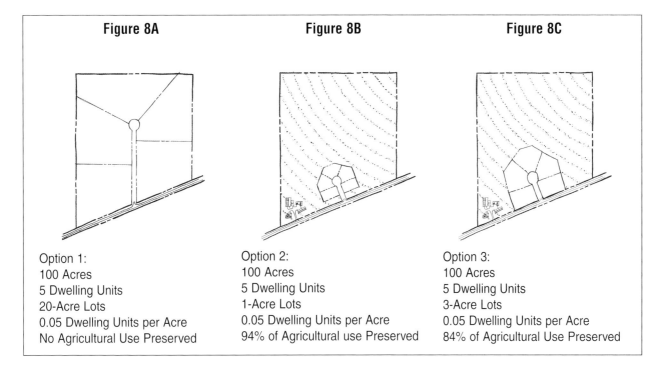

| **Figure 8A** | **Figure 8B** | **Figure 8C** |

Option 1:
100 Acres
5 Dwelling Units
20-Acre Lots
0.05 Dwelling Units per Acre
No Agricultural Use Preserved

Option 2:
100 Acres
5 Dwelling Units
1-Acre Lots
0.05 Dwelling Units per Acre
94% of Agricultural use Preserved

Option 3:
100 Acres
5 Dwelling Units
3-Acre Lots
0.05 Dwelling Units per Acre
84% of Agricultural Use Preserved

opments as an incentive. Note that the bonus only applies to Options 1 or 3 where the developer expects to achieve the maximum density.

7. *Transfer of Development Rights (TDR).* The traffic shed approach is complemented well by a voluntary transferable development rights (TDR) program. While the TDR program might be a traditional program in which land within a traffic shed (or across a jurisdiction encompassing more than one traffic shed) would be divided into sending areas and receiving areas. Sending areas are those that merit permanent protection from development because of their natural, historical, or agricultural value. Receiving areas are those that are deemed more suitable for development because they have few or no environmental constraints or because they are close to existing infrastructure and other developed areas.

TDRs take development pressure off sites that are remote from other development, providing them an opportunity to share in the development process while not creating a burden for the local government. They also permit dedicated farmers to sell their rights for development potential and keep farming a win/win situation for farmer, developer, and community. The author does not recommend this traditional program unless the county has a very strong capital program. TDR is a zoning strategy that generally increases complexity and is misunderstood .

With the traffic shed, an intradistrict transfer or noncontiguous development is the desired recommended form of TDR. Thus, two

The traffic shed system should not be adopted without other planning support. A capital improvements program, in conjunction with the traffic shed regulations, will steer investments and speculation to areas that have, or are planned to have, adequate facilities. While some areas may be suitable for development based on the present road system, others will need to be improved over time. In the long run, coordinating capital investment with planned growth areas will be as effective as an urban growth boundary system.

landowners in the same traffic shed and same zoning can concentrate development on a single property. For a family that wants to continue farming, TDR offers an option that provides income but does not force the family to sell the land. (See Figures 9A through 9D.) Used in conjunction with Option 6 (to cluster) and Option 3 (to reserve land), the landowner can sell development rights and reserve future development potential if road improvements are made that increase the density.

From the developer's point of view, the option to purchase development rights means they can market a larger project that combines the development potential of several properties. The increased density allows receiving sites to be used to their maximum potential.

These seven development options provide economic choices that account for land price, infrastructure costs, construction costs, and expected sales values. Because road costs are included in the equation, the traffic shed analysis harnesses market forces to reach nearly the same result as a growth management plan. The traffic shed approach is also geographically and topographically sensitive. Areas that are restricted by streams or topography have reduced densities. Streams can mean narrow bridges or even fords that reduce road capacity, and rugged topography can mean more curves and steep and narrow roads—again all reducing road capacity.

Areas that are far away from improvements also reflect the reduced development potential. The market will support development of new infrastructure by the developer only in areas where the costs justify the return. The community gets the new infrastructure and, thus, saves tax dollars.

The traffic shed system should not be adopted without other planning support. A capital improvements program, in conjunction with the traffic shed regulations, will steer investments and speculation to areas that have, or are planned to have, adequate facilities. While some areas may be suitable for development based on the present road system, others will need to be improved over time. In the long run, coordinating capital investment with planned growth areas will be as effective as an urban growth boundary system. Further, instituting a long-term investment strategy that is understood in the real estate community will steer development to the serviced areas. On the other hand, if capital improvements are unpredictable, real estate interests will be more speculative, and speculators will seek to promote capital investments that are beneficial to their interests rather than implementing the community plan.

The traffic shed has the advantage of not requiring a massive downzoning. In fact, the base zoning can be left unchanged, although greater flexibility will be achieved by modifying zoning to allow for clustering and development rights transfers. A capacity analysis results in a traffic-shed-specific overlay zone. And, while the use of a traffic shed system can have results as draconian as those offered by other growth management systems, the solutions it can provide respond to a number of commonly expressed concerns about other growth management and funding options.

1. *Taxes.* Use of a traffic shed regulation makes it less likely that higher taxes will be needed to pay for road improvements.

Figure 9A.

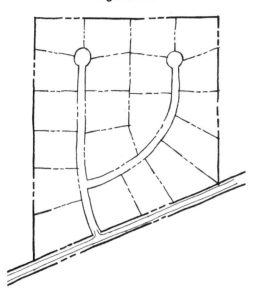

Parcel 1 Before Transfer of Development Rights

100 Acres
20 Dwelling Units
5-Acre Lots
0.20 Dwelling Units per Acre

Figure 9B.

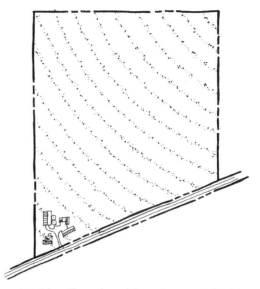

Parcel 1 After Transfer of Development Rights

100 Acres
1 Dwelling Units
100-Acre Lots
0.01 Dwelling Units per Acre

Figure 9C.

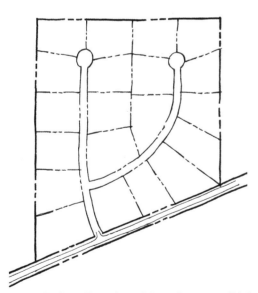

Parcel 2 Before Transfer of Development Rights

100 Acres
20 Dwelling Units
5-Acre Lots
0.20 Dwelling Units per Acre

Figure 9D.

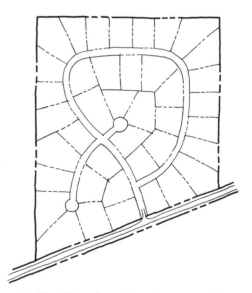

Parcel 2 After Transfer of Development Rights

100 Acres
40 Dwelling Units
<2.5-Acre Lots
0.40 Dwelling Units per Acre

Traffic sheds are not an agricultural preservation strategy. However, the incentive to cluster development and discourage sprawl can prolong agricultural uses. There is, of course, no assurance that land that is most restricted by the traffic shed will be good farmland, but, if the community uses the performance zoning approach, there can be incentives to protect resources and farmland.

2. *Capacity.* Most people can understand that, if government cannot afford to build new facilities, there needs to be a development limit that maintains the viability of existing infrastructure.

3. *Ability to Develop.* The traffic shed system always allows development, unlike the adequate facility ordinance in which local capacity problems can prohibit development.

4. *Equity.* The fair-share aspect of the system is more equitable that a first-come, first-served system that exists with a adequate public facilities program.

5. *Market Sensitivity.* The ability of a landowner to make improvements and thus increase density is a logical, market-oriented approach. If the developer can spend money to market a better product, the developer does so. On the other hand, if the improvement is too costly for the market place to support, there is no reason for government to subsidize a poor market decision to the detriment of those who are working within the market constraints.

The public also benefits from the application of the traffic shed system. The subsidy for landowners and developers who benefit from sprawl is eliminated. The community can rationally plan for expansion of services. Any improvements paid for by developers will reduce the need for local government to allocate scarce resources to the roads.

The traffic shed system described here addresses roads, but is, in fact, a performance standard that can address constraints on water supply, sewer, or soil limitations for sewer disposal equally well. In many parts of the nation, rural water districts or special districts that are not controlled by the zoning authority can be brought under control by such performance standards.

Traffic sheds are not an agricultural preservation strategy. However, the incentive to cluster development and discourage sprawl can prolong agricultural uses. There is, of course, no assurance that land that is most restricted by the traffic shed will be good farmland, but, if the community uses the performance zoning approach, there can be incentives to protect resources and farmland.

Overall, the technique has held up in both irregular transportation networks shaped by topography and in the grid systems found in agricultural areas. The system clearly works best in relatively rural areas. In urban areas, the linear nature of travel is absent. Trips move in multiple directions in a network, and, except in unusual conditions, the traffic shed is not applicable. A transportation model would have to be substituted for the traffic shed calculation.

It should also be noted that the traffic shed concept applies best to local roads. In many fringe areas, the capacity of the arterial system is also a problem. Since these arterials are typically state roads, either the state or county should require impact fees, or the county can just leave the improvement of these areas to the state.

A question the reader might have is If the concept is so good, why has it not been used more frequently? The traffic shed concept has not seen wide usage because almost nobody knows of its existence. The author developed it and used it where applicable on a few consulting assignments. In Woodford County, Kentucky, a joint project involving the author, Charles Siemon, and Bluegrass Tomorrow first got the traffic shed concept a wider exposure. Other than a little paragraph in *Planning,* there was no publicity for the traffic shed. The purpose of this volume is to provide the profession with the information so that in may more widely be used.

A CASE STUDY: WILLIAMSON COUNTY, TENNESSEE

The traffic shed technique was first used in Williamson County, Tennessee, in 1988. Major modifications have been made to the system since it was first implemented, but experience demonstrates that it works well as both a planning and a regulatory system. Specifically, over the past 10 years, the traffic shed methodology has been shown to be an effective means of controlling developments that would otherwise aggravate design and capacity problems on existing state and county roadways within the county.

Initially developed by Lane Kendig, Inc., and first adopted as a part of its zoning ordinance in 1988, Williamson County's traffic shed requirements have been updated, administered, and maintained since 1989 by Tocknell and Associates, acting as a consultant to the Williamson County Planning Commission.

Under Tennessee law, developments of five or more acres per single-family lot are excluded from the legal definition of a subdivision, and thus are exempt from local planning regulation. So, if the traffic shed methodology determines that suburban or urban development is not desirable, the default density is one single-family dwelling unit per five acres. To date, significant new development in Williamson County has not been considered to be economically feasible on five-acre lots.

In Williamson County, the density of residential development is either the basic zoning district density (e.g., 0.8 dwelling units per acre in the Suburban Estate district) or the density as determined from the highway capacity adjustment section (i.e., the traffic shed density). (See Figure 10 for a flowchart describing the process used to adjust highway capacity.) In turn, the traffic shed density is the more restrictive of either the arterial shed capacity or the collector shed capacity, expressed in trips per acre. The trips-per-acre calculation is easily converted to a corresponding land-use density (e.g., dwelling units per acre) through a table from the Institute of Transportation Engineers *Trip Generation* report. (See Table 1 for an example.)

If the traffic shed methodology applies only to collectors, all a developer has to do is to build a new collector to link up with the nearest arterial. This isn't very hard. But the arterials may not have the design or the capacity to handle the traffic that may

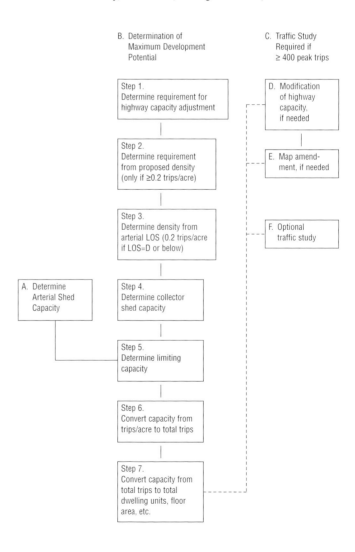

Figure 10. Highway Capacity Adjustment Flowchart, Williamson County, Tennessee, Zoning Ordinance, Section 5230

Table 1. Sample Trip Generation Rates

Land Use	Number of Peak-Hour Trips	Per (Type of Unit)
Agriculture	N/A	N/A
Residential		
Single-family detached	1.00	dwelling unit
Single-family attached	.85	dwelling unit
Multi-family, apartment	.70	dwelling unit
Mobile home	.60	dwelling unit
Institutional		
Outdoor institutional	N/A	N/A
Elementary school	.25	student
High school	.30	student
College/university	.40	student
Day care/nursery school	N/A	student
Hospital	1.30	bed
Nursing home	.30	bed
Commercial		
Office 0 to 100,000 gross square feet	2.85	1,000 gross square feet
Office >100,000 gross square feet	2.00	1,000 gross square feet
Medical office	5.00	1,000 gross square feet
Research center	2.50	1,000 gross square feet
Specialty retail	2.25	1,000 leasable square feet
Discount store	7.00	1,000 leasable square feet
Hardware store	5.20	1,000 leasable square feet
Shopping center 0-49,000 square feet	15.50	1,000 leasable square feet
Shopping center 50,000-100,000 square feet	9.30	1,000 leasable square feet

Figure 11. Portion of the Traffic Shed Map, Williamson County, Tennessee

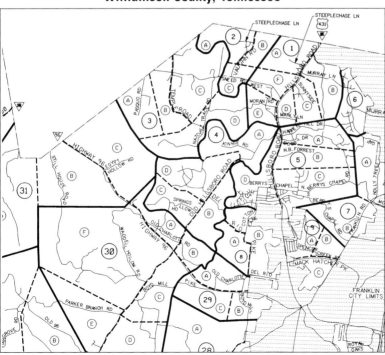

result from suburban development. So, Williamson County's traffic shed methodology requires an analysis of both the arterial and the collector system.

Figure 11 shows a portion of the Official Traffic Shed Map maintained by the Williamson County Planning Commission. On the map, each arterial shed is numbered and each collector shed is given a letter. Arterial sheds are aggregations of individual collector sheds. So "25C" would be the third collector shed within arterial shed 25. The letters are generally assigned to collector sheds in clockwise order around the center of the arterial shed.

The collector shed capacity is essentially the capacity of the designated roadway divided by the number of acres it serves. This is because the traffic shed divisions were initially set up so that no other traffic shed is likely to contribute significant traffic to the collector road in another traffic shed.

In contrast, many other traffic sheds may contribute traffic to a shed's arterial road, making the determination of the arterial shed capacity a little more tricky. The arterial shed capacity is derived through the weekday peak-hour traffic counts for the portion of the arterial road that will be affected by the proposed development. Data collected within the 12 months immediately preceding the analysis are acceptable (with the permission of the planning director) as are data from the state, county, or a county-recognized traffic consultant. (See Table 2 for an example of how Williamson County classifies its two-lane arterials and the correlating LOS; for arterials wider than two lanes, procedures from *The Highway Capacity Manual* may be used to determine LOS.) Using data provided by the county, the developer then determines the maximum number of trips permitted per acre at each level of service. (See Table 3.) If the arterial is wider than two lanes, the values from Table 2 are multiplied by 1.67 to determine the maximum number of permitted trips per acre.

Table 2. Highway Traffic Capacities

Roadway Classifications, Williamson County, Tennessee

	Green	Orange	Blue	Purple	Red
LOS A	250	200	150	100	75
LOS B	500	300	250	200	150
LOS C	850	550	500	375	250
LOS D	1,400	850	700	550	350

Of course, if a roadway serves a very large area (as most arterials do), the roadway cannot be shown to support any reasonable amount of new development even if it is overdesigned and overbuilt. For the number of acres, there will not be enough highway capacity to go around.

Williamson County's arterial shed methodology addresses this problem in two ways. First, development "upstream" from an arterial shed is represented by the volume of existing traffic that enters the arterial shed. As the volume approaches the capacity of the arterial roadway, permitted development densities within the arterial shed are reduced. If the arterial roadway is at full capacity before it enters the arterial shed, new development within that shed is practically prohibited.

Within arterial sheds, the permitted arterial shed densities were developed through a reverse application of the charts documented in a 1980 report of the Federal Highway Administration, *Land Use and Arterial Spacing in Suburban Areas.* The purpose of that report was to determine the number of arterial lanes per mile that would be needed in a given corridor, as a function of the permitted development density. For the Williamson

Table 3. Arterial Traffic Shed Capacities, Williamson County, Tennessee

Arterial Shed	Road Name	Acres	Class	Trips per Acre			
				LOS A	LOS B	LOS C	LOS D
1.	Hillsboro Rd.	4,403	Green	2.02	1.62	0.92	0.20
2.	Vaughn Rd.	1,981	Blue	1.86	1.50	0.96	0.20
3.	Temple Rd.	6,489	Orange	1.38	1.10	0.64	0.20
4.	Old Hillsboro Rd.	5,359	Blue	1.34	1.08	0.62	0.20
5.	Hillsboro Rd.	5,627	Green	1.82	1.46	0.84	0.20
6.	Murray Ln.	969	Blue	2.42	1.92	1.10	0.20
7.	Franklin Rd.	2,599	Green	2.32	1.86	1.06	0.20
8.	Del Rio Pike	2,075	Blue	1.86	1.50	0.92	0.20
9.	Mack Hatcher	1,697	Green	2.82	2.26	1.30	0.20
10.	Concord Rd.	3,784	Blue	1.60	1.28	0.74	0.20
11.	Nolensville Rd.	3,648	Green	2.16	1.72	1.00	0.20
12.	Split Log/S Donald	3,501	Purple	1.26	1.00	0.58	0.20
13.	Clovercrft/Nlnsvl Rd.	2,853	Blue	1.72	1.38	0.78	0.20
14.	Nolensville Rd.	1,588	Green	2.82	2.26	1.30	0.20
15.	Rocky Fork Rd.	2,244	Blue	1.86	1.50	0.92	0.20

County arterial traffic sheds, the same charts were used to determine the density of development that could be permitted (expressed in trips per acre) as a function of the size of the area served by each lane-mile of arterial. (See Table 4.) Once the capacities were determined based on the sizes of the arterial sheds, further adjustments were made to account for design factors that restricted or enhanced the capacity of each arterial roadway, as well as for the existing LOS on the roadway as it enters the arterial shed.

Taken as a whole, Williamson County's traffic shed requirements have effectively precluded development in the less accessible parts of the county. In most cases, new development simply has not occurred in these areas. Because the traffic shed densities are incorporated directly into the zoning ordinance, most developers can tell in advance whether it makes sense to proceed with a new development in a given area. With the traffic shed methodology in place, there is little or no market incentive to develop in areas of Williamson County that have sparse or poorly designed roadways.

At the southern end of the county, closest to the Saturn General Motors auto assembly plant and farthest from suburban Nashville, developers have avoided county planning restrictions by requesting annexation into the Town of Spring Hill, which is centered to the south of the county line in Maury County.

A better way to deal with the traffic shed restrictions has involved the use of the traffic study option. Because the traffic shed methodology applies mainly to small-scale residential development, the traffic shed chapter requires that a traffic impact study must be prepared for develop-

Table 4. Maximum Number of Peak-Hour Trips in Collector Sheds, Williamson City, Tennessee

Shed No.	Road Name	Zoning District	Acres	Highway Capacity	Trips per Acre
1-A	H'boro Valley Rd.	SE	982	1,100	1.12
B	Murray Lane	SE	1,043	1,400	1.34
C	Sunnyside Dr.	SE	663	1,400	2.11
D	Manly Lane	SE	393	700	1.78
E	Moran Rd.	E	323	1,400	0.20
		SE	318	1,400	4.20
F	Sneed Rd.	E	6	1,400	0.20
		SE	675	1,400	2.07
1-TOTAL	Hillsboro Rd.		4,403		
2-A	Steeplechase Ln.	SE	947	1,100	1.16
B	(NO COLLECTOR)	SE	487	***	0.20
C	Vaughn Rd.	E	92	1,400	0.20
		SE	455	1,400	3.04
2-TOTAL	Vaughn Rd.		1,981		
3-A	Pasquo Rd.	E	491	1,100	0.20
		SE	1,560	1,100	0.64
B	Sneed Rd.	E	199	1,400	0.20
		SE	1,133	1,400	1.20
C	Sneed Rd.	E	282	1,400	0.20
		SE	1,946	1,400	0.69
D	Temple Rd.	E	2,075	1,700	0.20
		SE	44	1,700	29.20
3-TOTAL	Temple Rd.		6,489		

ments expected to generate 400 or more peak-hour trips. For developments that generate fewer trips, a traffic study can still be prepared in order to suggest reasons for modifying the traffic shed requirements, based on the particular aspects of a given development and the design and capacity improvements that are being proposed.

Once the issues raised by the traffic shed analysis have been identified, they cannot be avoided in the traffic impact study. Nearly all of the traffic impact studies prepared for the Williamson County Planning Commission have included a section that addresses the traffic shed provisions of the county zoning ordinance. If there are deficiencies in either the design or the capacity of the roadway(s) that serves a given development, the study must address these deficiencies and show how the traffic shed requirements will be applied.

Finally, the county planning commission has the option, in most cases, to require some kind of mitigation or exaction in lieu of a complete restriction of development pursuant to the traffic shed requirements.

On county roads, the developer may be required to assume responsibility for the full cost of whatever improvements to the roadway system may be needed in order to support the development at its proposed intensity. Under a cost-recovery provision of the traffic shed chapter, the developer who paid the full cost of a given county highway improvement is entitled to recover a portion of the expense from subsequent developers whose properties benefit from the same improvement.

But the county also recognizes that a developer contribution would have little or no effect on the timing or design of a state highway. So, if the affected arterial is on the state highway system, the cost recovery provision is not enacted. Only an initial pro rata contribution is required toward the estimated cost of the necessary improvement(s) in order for a development to proceed.

In many cases, this requirement has been used as a starting point either for exactions or for in-kind improvements to the county highway system in lieu of a required cash contribution to the county on behalf of the state.

OTHER COMMUNITIES USING TRAFFIC SHEDS
Other communities where the traffic shed system has been used or seriously discussed include: Loudoun County, Virginia; New Castle County, Delaware; Miami County, Kansas; Woodford County, Kentucky; Fayette County, Kentucky; Nantucket, Massachusetts; and those in the area of interest for Blue Grass Tomorrow.

In Loudoun County, the rural areas of the Piedmont featured numerous unpaved, winding, and narrow state roads with very limited capacity. Landowners did not want the roads widened for fear that such widening would destroy the area's rural and historic ambiance. The traffic shed analysis, when applied to a number of study areas, showed that the existing three-acre lot size allowed by the zoning would exceed the capacity of the rural road network. The planning staff and planning commission were attracted to the traffic shed idea as a means of controlling development. Unfortunately, the county attorney was unwilling to risk an innovative approach. Some feared that the Virginia Supreme Court would reject the concept, which is what happened to a number of innovative land-use regulation efforts by nearby Fairfax County. It needs to be noted, however, that the court had upheld a similar performance-based approach with regard to governing development on the basis of soils for septic systems.

New Castle County first discussed the idea in the late 1980s, but a prodevelopment county board watered the plan down and did not implement major elements of the plan. In 1997, the county undertook a six-month comprehensive rezoning. The traffic shed, modified to use the transportation model as a base was considered. This is a rapidly growing county, and few roads had any significant capacity. It was determined that a traffic shed approach would have been generally impossible because none of the desirable infill areas would have had capacity to promote infill. In fact, even the current road impact standards made it impossible in that short time frame to map areas for desirable infill development.

In Miami and Woodford Counties, the concept has been used as an analysis tool in developing zoning proposals that would limit the total development capacity of the rural area through agricultural zoning. Woodford County was similar to Loudoun and Williamson Counties in the nature of the road system. The roads in Woodford are paved, but narrow, with poor horizontal and vertical alignment. In many cases there are stone walls close to the pavement edge. Traffic shed analysis was used as a rationale for revising the comprehensive plan to protect the rural character of the community.

Miami County was a demonstration of the application to the section line grids of the Midwest and West. Where the grid is on the fringe of a metropolitan area so that trips are highly directional, the traffic shed will work. In both these cases, the communities will rely on a downzoning to true agriculture densities to limit the growth to a level the existing roads can handle.

Nantucket is the only application in a generally urban area. The town center is very urban while the remainder of the island that is developed is suburban or estate in character. The system works in Nantucket because most of the roads radiate from Nantucket Center to the rest of the island. In most instances, major roads dead-end at the ocean. The LOS on the various roads is being evaluated for each of several plan alternatives; the existing zoning on the island will result in the failure of most main roads. The initial work involves a minimum of four development scenarios, each of which will be subjected to a traffic shed analysis of the impact of the land-use plan on traffic congestion. The plan is employing a computerized program, Strategic Analysis: Vision Evaluation System (SAVES), to evaluate the effects of development. The evaluation includes a traffic shed analysis of 12 planning areas. Because the vast majority of development potential on the island is attributable to the zoning bylaw that permits two principal structures per lot, it is unlikely that the traffic shed will be used as a zoning strategy since there is a much more obvious method of controlling development. Nearly 65 percent of the island's potential growth is contained in the allowance of a second dwelling on a lot. The most direct and effective growth management strategy for the island has to include the curtailment of the second dwelling. Complex rezoning or traffic shed zoning are more complex and do not focus on the majority of the potential growth.

The Bluegrass Regional Plan that was under preparation as this report went to press is proposed to be implemented by a "Rural Landscape Planning Tool." The tool is described as a simplified Geographic Information System (GIS) based on a mathematical model that allows for the analysis of development impacts. (See *Bluegrass Regional Plan, Bluegrass by Design, a Framework for a Regional Plan,* draft dated December 29, 1998.) A component of the tool is the rural road network capacity, based on a traffic shed analysis. There are two other components—a fiscal impact model and a development capacity model using GIS data. Charles Siemon of Siemon, Larsen, and Marsh is providing consulting services on the plan and tool for Bluegrass Tomorrow.

Fayette County, one of the Bluegrass Counties is also using the traffic shed. In recent years, Fayette County has been involved in a major update of its growth management plan. That work began with a major reassessment of the capacity of the urban growth area and a controversial expansion of that area. More recently, the effort has focused on the rural area. The urban growth management plan always showed the rural area as a green color, with a zoning of 10-acre lots. For a long time that was a sufficient barrier to rural development. In recent years there has been significant subdivision into these 10-acre parcels. The county began to assess the rural component of the plan with Siemon, Larsen, and Marsh. Initially, the plan proposed to use a combination of cluster zoning, transferable development rights, and the traffic shed to control growth in the area. As the plan evolved, the major horse farm owners decided they would rather have no development in their area. The traffic shed was used to evaluate development limits in a critical area of the county as a guide to setting densities. That analysis is now being completed for the entire county. The final plan will involve agricultural zoning and the purchase of development rights, negating the need for traffic-based controls.

SUMMARY

In summary, the traffic shed is a very useful planning and zoning concept with relevance for both rural and exurban areas. The traffic shed analysis can be applied as a planning tool to determine if there are carrying capacity constraints. It can also illustrate that there are real traffic problems even at low densities, an important planning consideration and capital improvement stumbling block. In zoning, the traffic shed may be used in conjunction with other strategies as part of a comprehensive growth management plan.

The carrying capacity nature of the system can be applied to rural water districts or even rural sewer lines. All of these public facilities can be organized into sheds served by a line, tank, or plant with finite capacities. Planning development in a rural area so that it does not exceed the capacity of roads or other public facilities enhances the ability of government to provide services in an era where public expenditures are often opposed. All too often, land-use plans or zoning for rural areas exceed the capacity of the community to provide infrastructure. The traffic shed and related zoning strategies are effective at controlling development.

The traffic shed analysis requires only readily available data and simple calculations. Obtaining the data and completing the calculations is far less expensive than attempting to develop a transportation model for the community. In rural areas, such analysis effectively evaluates the transportation impact of development and can identify the carrying capacity of both existing and improved roads.

Lastly, the traffic shed approach to regulations makes a great deal of sense. In an era when the courts are taking a harder look at local government regulations, the traffic shed approach, with its inherent flexibility, is a means of addressing difficult problems. It does not stop development. It

Planning development in a rural area so that it does not exceed the capacity of roads or other public facilities enhances the ability of government to provide services in an era where public expenditures are often opposed.

In an era when the courts are taking a harder look at local government regulations, the traffic shed approach, with its inherent flexibility, is a means of addressing difficult problems. It does not stop development. It simply requires private decisions to account for the costs they uniquely impose on local government.

simply requires private decisions to account for the costs they uniquely impose on local government. No landowner is rewarded at the expense of others since all share equally. The use of development rights transfers does not pay for development that the community limits; it is a tool to allow landowners additional choices. Thus, it avoids the legal and political problems of downzoning.

431 **Preparing a Landscape Ordinance.** December 1990. 26 pp. $28; PAS subscribers $14.

432 **Off-Street Parking Requirements: A National Review of Standards.** May 1991. 27 pp. $28; PAS subscribers $14.

434 **Personnel Practices in Planning Offices.** August 1991. 32 pp. $28; PAS subscribers $14.

435 **Electromagnetic Fields and Land-Use Controls.** December 1991. 20 pp. $26; PAS subscribers $13.

437 **Airport Noise Regulations.** May 1992. 16 pp. $26; PAS subscribers $13.

438 **Innovative Tools for Historic Preservation.** September 1992. 44 pp. $28; PAS subscribers $14.

440 **Staying Inside the Lines: Urban Growth Boundaries.** November 1992. 32 pp. $28; PAS subscribers $14.

441 **Affordable Housing: Proactive and Reactive Planning Strategies.** December 1992. 76 pp. $30; PAS subscribers $15.

442 **Capital Improvements Programs: Linking Budgeting and Planning.** January 1993. 56 pp. $30; PAS subscribers $15.

443 **Selecting and Retaining a Planning Consultant: RFQs, RFPs, Contracts, and Project Management.** February 1993. 44 pp. $28; PAS subscribers $14.

444 **Industrial Performance Standards for a New Century.** March 1993. 68 pp. $30; PAS subscribers $15.

445 **Manufactured Housing Site Development Guide.** April 1993. 46 pp. $28; PAS subscribers $14.

446 **Tree Conservation Ordinances: Land-Use Regulations Go Green.** August 1993. 108 pp. $32; PAS subscribers $16.

447 **Planning, Growth, and Public Facilities: A Primer for Local Officials.** September 1993. 32 pp. $28; PAS subscribers $14.

448/449 **The Transportation/Land Use Connection: A Framework for Practical Policy.** January 1994. 140 pp. $32; PAS subscribers $16.

450 **Preparing a Historic Preservation Plan.** March 1994. 58 pp. $30; PAS subscribers $15.

451 **Planning for an Aging Society.** April 1994. 64 pp. $30; PAS subscribers $15.

452 **Saving Face: How Corporate Franchise Design Can Respect Community Identity.** June 1994. 72 pp. $30; PAS subscribers $15.

453 **Presentation Graphics.** January 1995. 80 pp. $30; PAS subscribers $15.

454 **Design Review.** February 1995. 34 pp. $28; PAS subscribers $14.

455 **Neighborhood-Based Planning: Five Case Studies.** March 1995. 34 pp. $28; PAS subscribers $14.

456 **Traffic Calming.** July 1995. 28 pp. $28; PAS subscribers $14.

457/458 **A Guide to Wellhead Protection.** August 1995. 104 pp. $34; PAS subscribers $17.

459 **Bicycle Facility Planning.** October 1995. 44pp. $32; PAS subscribers $16.

460 **Preparing a Conventional Zoning Ordinance.** December 1995. 61 pp. $34; PAS subscribers $17.

461 **Performance Standards for Growth Management.** February 1996. 44 pp. $32; PAS subscribers $16.

462/463 **Modernizing State Planning Statutes: The Growing Smart™ Working Papers.** Vol. 1. March 1996. 190 pp. $24; PAS subscribers $12.

464 **Planners Salaries and Employment Trends, 1995.** July 1996. 25 pp. $28; PAS subscribers $14.

465 **Adequate Public Facilities Ordinances and Transportation Management.** August 1996. 80 pp. $34; PAS subscribers $17.

466 **Planning for Hillside Development.** November 1996. 50 pp. $32; PAS subscribers $16.

467 **A Planners Guide to Sustainable Development.** December 1996. 66 pp. $32; PAS subscribers $16.

468 **Creating Transit-Supportive Land-Use Regulations.** December 1996. 76 pp. $34; PAS subscribers $17.

469 **Gambling, Economic Development, and Historic Preservation.** March 1997. 56 pp. $32; PAS subscribers $16.

470/471 **Habitat Protection Planning: Where the Wild Things Are.** May 1997. 82 pp. $34; PAS subscribers $17.

472 **Converting Storefronts to Housing.** July 1997. 88 pp. $34; PAS subscribers $17.

473 **Subdivision Design in Flood Hazard Areas.** September 1997. 62 pp. $32; PAS subscribers $16.

474/475 **Online Resources for Planners.** November 1997. 126 pp. $34; PAS subscribers $17.

476 **Nonpoint Source Pollution: A Handbook for Local Governments.** December 1997. 127 pp. $32; PAS subscribers $16.

477 **Transportation Demand Management.** March 1998. 68 pp. $32; PAS subscribers $16.

478 **Manufactured Housing: Regulation, Design Innovations, and Development Options.** July 1998. 120 pp. $32; PAS subscribers $16.

479 **Principles of Smart Development.** September 1998. 113 pp. $32; PAS subscribers $16.

480/481 **The Growing Smart Working Papers, Volume 2.** December 1998. 269 pp. $28; PAS subscribers $14.

482 **Planning and Zoning for Concentrated Animal Feeding Operations.** December 1998. 44 pp. $32; PAS subscribers $16.

483/484 **Planning for Post-Disaster Recovery and Reconstruction.** December 1998. 346 pp. $34; PAS subscribers $17.

485 **Traffic Sheds, Rural Highway Capacity, and Growth Management.** March 1999. 24 pp. $26; PAS subscribers $13.

American Planning Association
Planning Advisory Service

Great Places in America:
Great Streets and Neighborhoods, 2007 Designees

American Planning Association

**Planning Advisory Service
Report Number 552**

In October 2007, the American Planning Association announced its first 10 Great Streets and 10 Great Neighborhoods in America. This Planning Advisory Service Report documents the success of those streets and neighborhoods. The response to the program resulted in unprecedented publicity about the program and APA—more than 130 television spots, 100 articles, and numerous blog entries. Because of this new initiative, people all across the U.S. are seeing the results of good planning and how planning can help create communities of lasting value.

PAS and APA thank the many planners, citizens, and officials who contributed to this first year of the program. PAS will produce a report each year documenting the designees from that year. In 2008, 10 more great streets and neighborhoods will be designated. In addition, APA will also designate 10 great public spaces.

For more about the Great Places in America program, please go to www. planning.org/greatplaces/. APA encourages you to become involved and nominate one of your favorite streets, neighborhoods, or public spaces.

Cover design by Lisa Barton; this report is printed on recyclable paper.

Cover photo of Michigan Avenue by The Greater North Michigan Avenue Association.

The Planning Advisory Service is a subscription service offered by the Research Department of the American Planning Association. Eight reports are produced each year. Subscribers also receive the *PAS Memo* each month and have use of the Inquiry Answering Service. W. Paul Farmer, FAICP, Executive Director and CEO; Sylvia Lewis, Director of Publications and Website; William Klein, AICP, Director of Research.

Planning Advisory Service Reports are produced in the Research Department of APA. James Hecimovich, Editor; Lisa Barton, Design Associate

© April 2008 by the American Planning Association.
APA's publications office is at 122 S. Michigan Ave., Suite 1600, Chicago, IL 60603.
E-mail: pasreports@planning.org
APA headquarters office is at 1776 Massachusetts Ave., N.W., Washington, DC 20036.